FR. BOB BE

M000042418

EVAN GEL IZA TION

A CHALLENGE *for the*
CATHOLIC
CHURCH

PUBLISHED BY THE
COMPANIONS OF THE CROSS
Ottawa, Ontario, Canada

COMPANIONS OF THE CROSS

Companions of the Cross
199 Bayswater Ave.
Ottawa, Ontario K1Y 2G5

www.companionscross.org

EVANGELIZATION
A CHALLENGE *for the* CATHOLIC CHURCH

by Fr. Bob Bedard, CC
Founder of the Companions of the Cross

Fourth Edition

Design by Shannon Kalyniak

ISBN 9781686826412

CONTENTS

1 OUR MANDATE: EVANGELIZE

Our gracious Father sent his divine Son, Jesus, to earth to accomplish our salvation. Without him, we would strive in vain to win it. The all-powerful Father, in perfect union from all eternity with the Son and the Holy Spirit, having no needs whatever, has incredibly desired to share his life with us. Jesus has made it possible for us to live now and forever as members of the divine household.

This is the Good News. And there is none to compare with it. The salvation the Lord Jesus has won is available to every man, woman and child who has ever lived. It is not to be earned, but is offered to us as a pure gift. We have only to accept it.

If we are baptized as infants, our parents choose this gift of salvation on our behalf. It remains for us to ratify this decision as we grow in wisdom, age, and grace before the Lord.

Before I can make my decision to choose Jesus as the Lord and Master of my life and follow him to the Father's house, the Gospel, the Good News, must be announced to me. St. Paul puts it well:

> *"How can they believe unless they have heard of him? And how can they hear unless someone preaches to them?"* (Rom. 10:14)

Jesus, in the Father's plan, has given this task of proclaiming the Good News of salvation to the Church. It is, in fact, the Church's number one mandate from the Lord. It takes precedence over everything else. All the good works we do, and there are many, must serve, and be in submission to, the Church's principal work.

We must organize for justice. We must labour for peace. We must lobby for life. We must reach out and serve all those in need—the hungry, the lonely, the alienated, the sick, the imprisoned, the abandoned, the despairing, and the addicted. The list is long. But, while all these are imperative to our mission from the Lord, one ministry stands first, head and shoulders above the rest: evangelization.

St. John Paul II made this abundantly clear again and again. He spoke a very clear word to the elders of the Church in Latin America at their landmark meeting in Puebla, Mexico, in 1980. He told them of his admiration for their efforts on behalf of social reform and encouraged them to carry it on. But he reminded them that their first obligation was to make sure that the Church put its work of evangelization above everything else.

In doing so, he was simply re-emphasizing the priority to which his predecessor, St. Paul VI, had recalled the Church.

Toward the end of his pontificate, St. Paul VI had written an encyclical on evangelization. Known as *Evangelii Nuntiandi*, it was the statement that, he said, he felt was his best. He was more pleased and enthused about it than about anything else he had ever written. His message was the essence of clarity: the Church's principal mission is to evangelize.

Of course, both of them were doing no more than being faithful to the mandate of the Founder himself, Jesus Christ, Son of God, Saviour.

There can be no question about it. Our highest priority as a Church must be the ministry of evangelization. And that mission is for all of us, not just for the bishops and pastors of the Church.

Yet for all of that, I'm convinced we don't do very much of it. We do lots of good things, and I know the Lord is pleased. But we don't do a lot of evangelizing.

I think we have forgotten how to do it. The simple technique of effective evangelization has slipped into the Church's sub-conscious and lies there largely dormant.

2 WHAT IS EVANGELIZATION?

The gospel is something I must choose to follow. It is not meant simply to be listened to and admired. It is not something primarily to study or talk about. I must do more than consider it. I must answer the call of the gospel with a resounding "yes". I must embrace it with my whole being.

I must be clear about the choice I make when I decide to accept the Lord's call to life. It involves making Jesus the Lord of my life and entering thereby into a personal relationship with him. I begin to know him in a deeper and more intimate way.

Evangelization, therefore, is the process whereby a person hears the gospel, embraces it fully, makes Jesus Lord of his life and gets involved in a lively, intimate and ongoing relationship with him.

St. Paul VI would agree with this definition. In the encyclical mentioned, he spoke of the "radical conversion" to the Lord that the gospel requires (*Evangelii Nuntiandi* 10). He spoke of the necessity of the "...profound change of mind and heart" that full evangelization involves.

St. John Paul II said the same thing. Evangelization calls, he taught, for a deliberate "acceptance of the Good News" (Puebla, Mexico, 1980). When he added, "God's action requires our response" (Ibid) he just about said it all.

Both St. Paul VI and St. John Paul II understood fully what evangelization is all about and taught it with consistent clarity. But we're not doing it. We're not really evangelizing. This is not to put us down. As a Church, we Catholics are doing much that is good. We're good teachers and servants. We celebrate well the mysteries of the Lord. But evangelization is not something we are very good at. With some bright and shining exceptions, we just don't know how to do it.

For the most part, when we preach, we explain Scripture and teach. We give information. We intellectualize, reflect, discuss and suggest food for thought. All these are good and commendable. But we don't often evangelize. The pulpit is designed as the principal platform for evangelization. We must begin again to use it as such.

The classroom, as well, has the potential to be a powerful instrument in the proclamation of the gospel. But we don't evangelize there either. Much good work goes on in our schools. There may be a number of dedicated teachers, principals, administrators, trustees, and others making a good impact on our children and young people. But, sad to say, most of the youngsters who graduate from our school system have not made a firm decision to follow Jesus and embrace the truth of his gospel. They are not being evangelized.

Basically, both in the pulpit and classroom, we give answers to questions people are not asking. We have the cart before the horse. We give information about the Scriptures, the teachings of the Church, the Commandments, the Sacraments, Church history, theology, modern Church problems, and a number of other things as well. This may be all to the good, but it isn't evangelization.

By and large, the experience our Catholic people receive in our churches and schools is a positive one. But it lacks the life-changing power that the Lord would endow it with if only we would evangelize in the full sense of the word. We have to begin again to understand what evangelization is and how it works.

Because we have not been doing much actual evangelizing, we have had to face the consequences. We have been witnesses in the last twenty years or so to a distressing exodus from our parish churches. Every little while we are confronted with the latest poll which serves up statistics that are anything but reassuring. Each tally reports a somewhat smaller regular church attendance among Catholics than the previous poll.

Not so long ago I heard a bishop describe the situation in his diocese. He told us that twenty-five years ago on the average Sunday close to 80% of the Catholic people would be in church. Now, he said, it would be closer to 15%! The statistics in his diocese are probably more typical of the Church in North America than most of us would like to recognize.

In our search for the reasons for this unfortunate situation we tend, I'm afraid, to rely on geographic, demographic, sociological, psychological and other like factors. We are baffled, blame the spirit of the age, and hope the behavioural sciences or some new theological insight can bail us out.

I would suggest a much more basic explanation. Many of our people have fallen away from what we call the "practice" of their faith for the simple reason that they were never properly or fully evangelized in the first place.

Because we do not evangelize, we are paralyzed by false optimism. We are somehow convinced that the Church will flourish if we can just get our people to Mass on Sunday, see long lines of regular communicants, baptize and confirm all the children, run a large Catholic school system, and keep our parishes humming with activity.

This is false optimism. And it paralyzes us. It prevents us from coming to grips with the real problem. It keeps us from asking what I believe to be the vital question: Are we really evangelizing? I am convinced the answer is "no" and would urge and beg us to face the issue and do something about it.

I hope I'm not sounding critical. That is not my intention. I am Catholic to the very roots of my being. I believe the Catholic Church to be the Church of the ages, touching historically our blessed Saviour, Jesus himself. I believe it to be the fullest expression of what the Lord wants his people to be and the most faithful to the Father's blueprint for the Body of Christ on earth. I have profound respect for the non-Catholic brothers and sisters and I have confidence the Lord is going one day to bring us together. In fact, I believe he is moving powerfully to do it now. And I know the Catholic Church is far from perfect and has much renewal and purification ahead of it before we can enter into the union of his people that the Lord has in mind.

But I love the Church. I call it the "sleeping giant". Once we begin to rediscover what it means to evangelize and to undertake a large-scale revival of this ministry, I see the Church waking up and coming explosively alive to the point where it, with the power of the Holy Spirit, will shake the earth and the nations with its dynamic presence.

3 THE THREE-STEP DYNAMIC

Let us delay no longer in getting practical. The dynamic is quite simple. There are three steps to it.

STEP ONE: Proclamation of the Gospel.
This is something that the minister of evangelization does, whether priest, religious, or lay person. The proclamation is done in such a way as to elicit the appropriate response. It has to be made clear that God's invitation to life is one that must be embraced fully. Jesus is to be chosen as Lord. The person being evangelized must be clear that he is called to hand his life over totally to the Lord.

STEP TWO: Response.
The hearer has to make a conscious decision to throw his lot in with Jesus and, in a proper spirit of repentance, fully accept the Lord's design for his life. Jesus Christ is chosen as Lord.

STEP THREE: Direct action of God.

The Lord moves the person from within in such a way that the one who has responded to the call knows it.

Please note that, while steps one and two are human—things we do—step three is divine. It is something God does. To put it another way, evangelization is something that we begin, but that God finishes. When we announce the Gospel the way we're supposed to, and when the proper response is made, he supplies the power.

A person who is touched by the hand of God, who senses his presence and his power in a new way, is bound to be significantly transformed. Having experienced the Lord himself, he now knows him in a way he didn't before. He is evangelized. It is as simple as that.

I find that many people have difficulty believing that this is really all there is to effective evangelization. It's as though they are saying, "It can't be that simple. There must be more to it than that." Why do we think it has to be complicated? The call of the Gospel is very straightforward. The complications are ours.

Others have difficulty with the notion that God himself actually intervenes in tangible ways. I must confess I had the same problem until I saw and experienced the Lord's power myself.

Without meaning to be offensive or flippant, my reply to objectors is: "Don't knock it. Try it. It works." How do I know? I've seen it. Again and again.

When I "discovered" the uncomplicated dynamic of evangelization, it seemed so elementary that I began to wonder why I hadn't realized this before.

Scripture is amazingly clear on the matter. The Lord says through the prophet Jeremiah:

> *"If you seek me with all your heart, I will allow you to find me."* (Jer. 29:13)

When a person reaches out to the Lord, the Lord moves in. He doesn't hide.

The writer of Psalm 37, my favourite psalm says:

> *"Commit your life to the Lord. Trust in him, and he will act."* (Ps. 37:5)

Again, the action of God becomes tangible when his call to life is responded to fully.

John, the beloved disciple, writes:

> *"To those who accepted him, he gave power to become children of God."* (John 1:12)

The Book of Revelation quotes Jesus himself:

> *"I stand at the door and knock. If anyone will but open the door, I will come in, sit down at table and have supper with him."* (Rev. 3:20)

James puts it perhaps the most simply of all.

> *"Draw close to God,"* he says, *"...and he will draw close to you."* (Jas. 4:8)

The dynamic seems not only clear, but consistent. The person who, having heard the Lord's call to come close to him, responds decisively, will experience the Lord's power and presence in an unmistakable way. This process is at the very heart of real evangelization.

Let me try to put it into my own words. God the Father has taken considerable initiative on our behalf. He has created us, breathed us forth into life. He has invited us to share his own life, to dwell with him forever as members of his household. He has sent his divine Son, Jesus, to earth to become one of us (forever, at that) and, through his saving death, Jesus has made eternal life possible for us. He has made the Holy Spirit available to us to provide us with all the power and resources we need to respond effectively to his invitation to life. And he continues, through the Spirit, to prompt us to say "yes" to becoming disciples of Jesus.

That's a lot of initiative.

Now it's our turn. The call to discipleship, to membership in the kingdom of God, comes to us from Jesus. His call to "Come, follow me" is directed to all people of all time. We're called to make ourselves fully available to the Lord. But it's our choice. We're free to accept or reject the invitation. It calls for a decision. We were made over to the Lord at Baptism. This needs to be ratified by each of us. And, if we've never deliberately done this before, there's really no better time than right now.

Once we make a conscious, considered decision to place ourselves under the Lordship of Jesus, God then makes his own sovereign move. The Father, through his Holy Spirit, begins to bestir us from within, to transform us. We are introduced to the realm of authentic spiritual or religious experience. We have been evangelized.

Our response opens the door of our lives to the Lord, and frees him to have his way with us, to move us from within and transform us. But how do we go about it?

4 THE LORD'S CALL

I have not always understood evangelization the way I believe I understand it now. Although I am not so engaged at present, many of my years in the priesthood were spent teaching in a Catholic high school while acting as a weekend assistant in a variety of parishes. My approach for most of that time was a fairly standard one, the approach I perceive practically all of us Catholics use.

In my Religion classes and in the pulpit, I explained, I gave information, I asked rhetorical questions designed to get people to think. It was a moderate success at best. I do know that a distressing number of my students quit going to church not long after leaving high school. They had never, of course, been truly evangelized.

In any case, in 1975, my experience in a Holy Spirit seminar changed my approach. I asked the Lord to help me to be more a man of prayer and I trusted him to answer. Nothing fancy, just a bit of help to pray better. Others prayed with me that my request be honoured by God. And it was. I began rather quickly to sense a real hunger for prayer and at times just couldn't wait to get to that daily quiet time with the Lord. For me, it was a most dramatic answer to a prayer.

I began to understand what I have called the Lord's own dynamic, the dynamic that is at the very heart of real evangelization. When I make a specific response to a specific call from God, he usually gives a very specific answer. He has power to move me from within, to transform me, to enlighten and direct me, provided that I let him. The Lord's call to each of us to pray is quite clear and specific. My response to that call was equally specific and quite sincere. And his moving within me was likewise unmistakable.

For me, it was a discovery. Others may have been well aware of it, but I must confess it had escaped me completely, had gone right over my head. I had certainly experienced God's action in my life before, but I don't think I really understood how it happened. Now I felt I understood.

It didn't take me long to come to the conclusion that my approach to ministry needed to change. I was well convinced that, if the Lord's call could be clearly presented to my students and to the people in the pews as an invitation to respond to, people could easily begin to experience God's power in their lives in ways that would transform them, bring them more alive in faith, and take them into an intimate relationship with the Lord himself. They could have the same kind of experience of the Lord that I had received. If they would simply reach out to God as he continues to reach out to them, the Lord would significantly change them.

If they would do their simple part, he would do the rest.

Therefore, my approach changed. In every class and in every homily, I began to confront the people with the notion that God wanted to deal with them and would do so, if they would but move toward him and allow him to have his way. And, to put it frankly, it worked. I saw the Lord's dynamic in action before my very eyes. I saw people change, saw them come alive in faith, saw the Lord work within them.

So clear, so powerful, yet so simple was it to me that I have become convinced that we, as a Church, all need to minister in the same way. And nobody has been able to talk me out of it.

5 LORD, IF YOU'RE REAL, SHOW ME!

My work at the high school included, as it had for several years, the senior Religion program. I had been accustomed to changing the program just about every year, trying every approach I would read about, hoping to come upon something that would catch the students' interest. At the time of my "discovery", I had been entitling the course, "The Problems of the Modern Church". It was a survey, a wide range of topics, covering just about everything controversial that was going on in the Church at the time. The students affected a mild and polite interest.

In 1975, however, I decided to use what I now believe to be the Lord's own program and strategy in order to give him a chance to do what I had never really been able to do—change people's hearts.

I began to present to the students the full challenge of the gospel—to step forward and hand their lives over to the Lord. This was certainly new. Previous to that, my approach had been to water the Lord's message down in the hope that the students would be able to accept some of it. Now I was inviting them to meet the Lord on his terms: total surrender.

The people I was dealing with were seventeen to nineteen years of age. Most of them had been in Catholic schools right from the start. Yet their actual understanding of Church teaching was amazingly scanty and inaccurate. It wasn't that they hadn't been well taught. It was simply that they had been given answers to questions they had never asked and, of course, couldn't remember the answers. The cart was before the horse.

At any rate, at this point in their lives, most of them were quite unsure of what they believed. The average senior high school student, I felt, was a person who was wondering if God was real. Some of them were sure he was. Others seemed equally as sure he wasn't, or that it didn't matter anyway. But most of them were somewhere in between, just not sure how real God was.

They had heard a lot about him, but had never really met him. In their classes and parishes, God had generally been treated as a definition and Jesus as a historical person. They were hoping he was real, but figured they didn't have enough actual evidence to substantiate it.

I would begin by assuring them that their position was understandable, but that the Lord himself was very anxious to convince them he was real. I told them God was tired of being a spectator in their lives and wanted very much to be a participant. And I gave them examples of how I had witnessed him intervening in human situations. I had dozens of stories by this time, all of them true. I suggested they give the Lord a chance to reveal himself to them.

I quoted for them again and again the Lord's word through the prophet Jeremiah:

> *"If you seek me with all your heart, I will allow you to find me."* (Jer. 29:30)

I even paraphrased it and suggested something like the following: "Lord, I'm hearing that you're real, that you love me, and that you want to be a part of my life. But I'm not sure of any of this. If you are real, please show me somehow. Because, if you are real and do care, it's going to make a great difference in my life, and I've got to know."

One of the great consolations in teaching school is that occasionally a student will actually listen to what the teacher says. And not only that, but some of them will even do what the teacher suggests. Some of the young people began to seek the Lord, began to say to him: "Lord, if you're real, show me." And it began to happen. He showed them.

What was going on? They were beginning to be "evangelized".

It is my firm opinion that if the Lord can touch the life of an older teenager, he can do it to anybody. The average young adult is under incredible pressure from the world, pressure to conform as well as to be a "success". He has vocational and educational decisions to make, to say nothing of the moral questions that become more intense and immediate.

Relationships are unsure and delicate, and yet so very important. To put it mildly, he has a lot on his mind. In addition to that he is probably as close to his physical best as he'll ever be.

In a sense, the world is almost at his doorstep.

If the Lord can break into such an appealing, busy and complicated life, he can do it, I believe, for anybody.

Other then the obvious interest a number of the young people were betraying in class, the first inkling I had that something significant was happening was during an interview with one of the young men. He had asked to see me. Since I was an accredited and veteran member of the Guidance Department, this was not unusual.

He began talking about a problem his sister was having, a relationship that I could see was quite out of order as he described it to me. He was very concerned about her, he told me. He had spoken to her about it and had been told to mind his own business. He had spoken to the other party involved, and had come close to being "punched out", as he put it, for his trouble.

Then he told me he had been praying about it, had not seen the Lord get involved in it as yet, but, he said, he had a sense the Lord was going to do something about it soon.

I nearly fell off my chair. "Good heavens!" I thought, "He's talking my language." I didn't know him all that well, but I considered him a good and decent chap. However, I was not expecting to hear what I'd heard.

Recovering my composure, I remarked that he seemed to have a rather lively faith. With an admirable modesty and shy smile, he avowed this to be true. Then I asked him if he'd always had that kind of faith.

His reply confirmed everything I felt the Lord had been teaching me about evangelization. "Oh no, Father," he replied. "In grade eleven, I packed it in altogether. I decided that religion was just a myth, a bunch of garbage. I quit praying and going to church, the whole bit. But I heard you say in class when we started this year that, if we weren't sure of God, we should give him a chance to convince us he was there and cared about us. So, every night before I went to bed, I started to say, 'Lord, if you're real, show me!' Before long, he showed me. Now I know."

So, there it was. Right before my eyes, the Lord was giving me the evidence that I was on the right track, that what I was calling his "dynamic" was, in fact, just that. I felt he was making it very clear to me that I was to continue to evangelize in the same way and that he would honour this by touching hearts. And I continued to do it, both in and out of school, and the evidence kept piling up.

The young man was only the first of a long string of people who opened their hearts to the Lord and could give testimony to God's action in their lives.

But the most dramatic thing I saw the Lord do in this way over the years occurred in the life of one of the young women.

She was bright and pleasant, very involved in the Canadian History class that I taught, but very quiet in Religion. One day she asked if she could come to talk to me. She wasted no time getting to the point. She said: "You know, you intrigue me. I never before heard anybody talk the way you do in Religion class. Do you really believe the things you're saying?"

She was talking about the things I said I had seen God do. When I told her that indeed I did believe them, she replied, "I thought you'd say that. You seem very convinced. Well, I respect your beliefs, but as for me, I don't believe in God at all."

Then she told me why. She had had an incredibly rough time as a young teenager and had been able to survive it only through the patient faithfulness of her parents. She said: "You see, I don't think it's possible that there could be any God who was supposed to be good who could let a young girl go through the hell I had to go through." I could certainly understand what she was saying and sympathize with her position. There are really no good reasons not to believe in God, but the one that's closest to making sense is the one she talked about.

I suggested to her that, though she didn't believe in God, God still believed in her and wanted her to be a full-fledged member of his Kingdom. I further suggested that she give him a chance to reveal himself to her by addressing herself to him, taking a step in his direction.

She said, "But, how can I address him, if I don't believe he's there?" I responded with, "Suppose he is there, what have you got to lose?" After much discussion, she agreed to give it a try.

She returned twice more during the course of the school year. Each time, I could see she was resisting the Lord for all she was worth and wanted only to discuss the intellectual objections to his existence. I tried to explain to her that she could not reason her way to faith, that God was too big to fit into her head, and that he revealed himself to a person's heart. Each time she left reluctantly to pursue the Lord.

The school year ended, and I spent July at a Scripture institute in San Antonio, Texas. When I returned home the first week of August, among the bills and circulars in my mail was a short letter from her. It went in part something like this:

"Thank you for the time you took with me during the past year. I thought you might like to know what has happened with me. I continued to seek the Lord as you had urged me. Well, he has now revealed himself to me. I know now that he's real and loves me. I just hope I can get to know him better."

The Lord had done it again.

This is how evangelization works. It's a simple dynamic. Our task is nothing more than to put the word out there and let the Lord go to work. He's the one who touches people and turns them around. It's real, it's powerful, and it lasts.

There is no more profound truth than that the Lord speaks to the heart. In fact, very often the head can get in the way. The more intelligent a person is, the greater tendency he has to rely on himself and to believe he can reason everything out, including the existence of God. He often reduces the Lord to an academic concept.

This was driven home to me one day with a great emphasis in a conversation with a former student. He was reminiscing about his high school days and reflecting on my Religion class (pre-1975).

He referred to my lesson on the proof for the existence of the soul. He said: "You made it all sound so logical and compelling. Even the diagram you put on the board made sense. But, you know, it didn't make a particle of difference in the way I live my life. It didn't change me in any way. That didn't happen until, much later, I turned my life over to the Lord."

It is the Lord's own action that makes the difference. Until he acts in my life, I don't really know him and have difficulty entering into a relationship with him. It is through the ministry of evangelization fully and properly carried out, that all this happens.

As time went by, the testimonies began to pile up. I should have opened a file.

One big fellow, a stalwart on the football team, found the Lord as well. His parents having separated, he had been living with his father, and hadn't been to church since grade seven. He used to sit in the last row of the Religion class and tip his chair back as he listened to my words. It was hard to tell what he was thinking, but his face usually had a rather quizzical look about it.

That year, the class organized its own weekend retreat. Persuaded by a couple of his friends, but against his better judgment, he went.

I'll never forget his reaction. Monday morning after class, he stayed behind and caught me before I left the room. I had not been at the retreat or been connected with it in any way.

"Father," he said, getting right to the point. "I went on that retreat. You know those things you've been telling us in class about how real God is and how he wants us to know him and wants to get involved in our lives?" He went on as he loomed over me and became quite animated, "Well, it's all true."

He had been evangelized. He had turned his life over to the Lord and the Lord had touched him. He's never been the same since.

At a similar exercise when she had been in grade eleven, the life of one of the girls had been turned around completely. She testified to us in class that she had fallen into bondage to both drugs and alcohol as a young teenager and was heading down a path to total destruction.

On the weekend (she went, she said, just to get some of her friends "off my case") she had come to a crisis point and cried out to God. She told us the words she had used: "God, if you're real, come into my life now, and help me to start again."

She had a powerful experience of the Lord's presence, love and power right on the spot. That was many years ago. She has been an extremely active member of the Church and a beautiful witness to the Lord ever since.

As time went on, it began to occur to me that I might encourage more of the students to reach out to the Lord if I provided them with a structure within which they could vocalize a concrete response to the Lord's call. Accordingly, toward the end of the school year, we would have a special Eucharist to which were invited all those who wanted to make a public consecration of their lives to the Lord. This usually drew from twenty-five to forty percent of the class.

I was into my fourth year of this program when I began to wonder just how effective the Mass of Commitment, as we called it, was. After all, it happened at the end of the students' final high school year, after which they would scatter to the four winds. Were they persevering with the Lord or was it just a passing experience? I puzzled over it.

Since it was a bit of a hassle to organize it, and since I didn't need any unnecessary hassles, I was considering not doing it the fourth time around. Because I was unsure of what course to follow, I took it to the Lord in prayer, a practice to which I was now becoming accustomed.

I told him I was not inclined to go ahead with the structured response because I simply didn't have enough evidence as to its effectiveness and, unless I had some pretty strong indication from him to the contrary, I would not be repeating the procedure again. But, of course, if he wanted it done, I would be more than happy to do it.

Within a few hours, I received a phone call I wasn't expecting. It was a young man, a former student, asking if he could come over and talk to me. Although I knew him well enough and always considered the two of us to be on good terms, I had never had any kind of conversation with him. In fact, I wasn't sure if I had seen him even once in the almost three years it had been since his graduation from high school. I wondered what he could want to see me about.

He was having difficulty, he told me when he arrived, with a decision he had to make. He was in his third year of science and was wondering if he should apply for medicine. This type of vocational decision was something I was very used to helping students with. My work in the Guidance Department included a lot of that. I anticipated, with that disclosure, therefore, a very familiar type of interview. But I was wrong.

He began to talk about how he had been praying to the Lord for guidance. I was pleased and edified. Then he said he as yet had no real sense of what God was saying to him, but that he had confidence he would soon receive the wisdom he needed to make his decision. "There's one thing for sure, Father," he said, "I don't want to do anything except what God wants me to do."

I was getting much more interested now in the conversation. In fact, I was fascinated. Here was another of my students talking my language.

But he wasn't finished, not by a long shot. He said something else that just knocked me right out. "Father," he said, "I know this is going to sound crazy, and I'm even embarrassed to say it. But, although I haven't sensed the Lord saying anything to me about my decision, the one thing I was sure he was telling me was to come and talk to you. It sounds pretty silly, I know, but that's the reason I'm here."

I was momentarily speechless, but recovered quickly enough to tell him how impressed I was with his faithfulness and perseverance in pursuing the Lord's will. Then I asked him the question I was by this time getting used to asking. "Tell me," I said, "have you always had this kind of strong and lively faith?"

His answer was the type I was getting used to hearing as well. "Oh no, Father," he replied. "Don't you remember? When I was in high school, my faith was pretty ordinary. But I was in the senior class the first year you started having that Mass of Commitment. I wasn't going to go, but I wound up going anyway. I turned my life over to the Lord that night and I've never looked back."

Then he put it in a way I've never forgotten. "It was after that night," he said, "that I never felt I had to be 'cool' again." That was the way I had remembered him—good, but pretty 'cool'.

Do you see what the Lord was saying to me? I had told him I was going to drop the structured response to his call unless I had a clear indication from him to the contrary. Well, my young visitor's testimony was my clear indication. He didn't know why God had sent him to me, but I certainly did.

It's as though the Lord was saying to me: "So you thought that the Eucharist of Commitment was your idea, eh?

Well actually, it was my idea. It's good to help people respond to my call by providing them with some formula. So, stay with it. Don't give it up."

I could add dozens of stories very much the same as these, from parishes as well as classrooms. I include them, not to show how clever I have become, but to illustrate a truth that I believe to be crucial to the ministry of the Church. We must call people to hand their lives over to the Lord, to commit themselves totally to his purposes. We must evangelize in the full sense of the word.

In this, I feel I'm not exactly a voice crying in the wilderness. The popes of recent times have all been saying exactly the same thing.

6 PUTTING IT INTO PRACTICE

How do we become effective evangelizers? There are, it seems to me, three principal avenues that are wide open to us: preaching, teaching and witnessing. We'll take them one at a time.

PREACHING:

Our preaching has to change. We have to begin to call people to decision. The basic, underlying challenge of Jesus' Gospel call is to consecrate everything to him, to make him the Lord of our lives. It involves our giving over to the Lord any attempt to exercise control. It is a total surrender.

A young man of my acquaintance put it as well as I have ever heard it. He said, "Once Jesus is perceived for what he really is, only one response makes any sense at all—total. Anything else is insane."

Many find it frightening. That's natural. The world tells us to get everything in our lives under control and to keep it that way. And we are, whether we like to admit it or not, rather thoroughly brainwashed by the world. Giving the Lord control demands almost a step into the unknown. And yet, there is every reason to trust the Lord. We have not only his word that he will never abandon us, a word that he has never broken, but we have the testimony of thousands of witnesses as well. Those who have committed themselves entirely to the Lord can attest to his complete reliability.

This is what evangelization is all about. The one who evangelizes attempts to call forth from the listeners this total response to the Lord. Until such a response is made in a person's life, he cannot properly be said to have been evangelized.

Our preaching *must* change. Our priests and deacons *must* become evangelists in the pulpit. I am convinced our clergy are not there yet. We don't often call forth the response that will open people's hearts to allow the Lord to move in and deal with them in a way that only he can.

Every homily must be a calling forth, must be evangelistic. While the basic call of the Lord is for the total surrender of our lives, while this is the "big" decision, there are other facets to the gospel summons as well. There are other, or follow-up, decisions to be made.

Jesus calls for a number of other very specific responses; to repent, to forgive, to pray, to fast, to love, to serve the poor, to submit to God's order in our lives, to give alms, to celebrate his death and rising, and to yield to the promptings of the Holy Spirit. There are others. Every homily, if we are being faithful to the assigned readings, will deal with one or more of these responses. We must call our listeners to say "yes" to whatever the Lord's call is. It is ongoing evangelization, or the "New Evangelization" the Pope and the Bishops have been calling for.

The point is that when a person hears God's call and responds to it by way of a conscious decision or deliberate action, God himself moves in and becomes tangibly involved in the person's life. Until we can get our people to answer the Lord's call, they will tend to remain unevangelized and be what far too many of our statistical Catholics are—occasional church-goers or, at best, uninvolved spectators.

We must continually confront them with one of the most basic truths about God—that he wants to be a participant in their lives and is tired of being merely an observer. As we evangelize from our pulpits, our preaching must focus much more fully on Jesus than it ordinarily does. We must become more comfortable in speaking his name.

In *Evangelii Nuntiandi*, St. Paul VI made it clear: "There is no true evangelization if the name...of Jesus is not proclaimed." And again: "To evangelize is first of all to bear witness...to Jesus Christ." He says, too, that the properly evangelized are "...those who by faith have acknowledged and *accepted Jesus Christ as Lord*." This comes from the highest authority in the Church, the chief shepherd of God's people on earth, the successor of Peter, the Bishop of Rome, the Vicar of Christ himself! If only we would hear his word to us and obey it!

St. John Paul II continued to say the same thing. In one of his weekly messages in 1979, he urged the assembly to "...walk toward Christ. He alone is the solution to all your problems." (St. Peter's, Rome, 1979) In 1978 he had said, "...to seek, love, and bear witness to Jesus—this is your commitment. These are the instructions I leave you." (St. Peter's, Rome, 1978) In his memorable visit to Canada in September 1984, he repeated again and again that "Jesus is the answer to all your problems. Look nowhere else."

Our people should walk out of their parish churches with the name of Jesus ringing in their ears. The pulpit is the principal platform for carrying out the Church's prime mission. It needs to be converted completely to that purpose.

TEACHING:

We have many opportunities to teach. We have adult education programs. We have catechism classes for children and teenagers, both in Catholic schools and parish facilities. And we have endless opportunities to teach our children at home.

Our teaching, like our preaching, can and must become evangelistic. Everything that can be said about the preaching can be said as well about the opportunities we have to teach. People must be called to respond to the gospel message so that the Lord himself can touch their lives. In fact, unless a person opens the door to his life the Lord does not move in. He is polite in the extreme. He never forces himself upon anybody. Unless we evangelize properly, the doors of people's hearts will not open as widely as they might, and God's action in their lives will not be as powerful as he himself wants it to be. It will be difficult, among other things, to teach them. They will not have that hunger to know more about the Lord, a hunger that he places there himself when they open up their lives to him.

In fact, unless we thoroughly evangelize the people first, I believe we have to question seriously our ability to teach them with any effect at all.

I feel I know what I'm talking about here. I taught high school for nineteen years. I was part of a teaching staff, a number of whom were priests, who had a deep concern for the spiritual welfare of the students, as well as everything else, and who were very dedicated to the task. Our stated goal was the overall development of the young people with a special effort to help them come alive in faith. Through no lack of effort or good will on our part or on the part of the students, we fell far short.

And we tried everything. We used every program we could get our hands on. We switched textbooks continually. We used audio and video aids. We had discussion and sharing groups. We celebrated the liturgy. We had days of recollection, retreats, seminars, workshops, weekend experiences.

I would not want to suggest that these were without effect entirely. Good things did happen. But our goal was far from being realized. Very few of our young people came powerfully alive in the Lord. In fact, the distressing reality was that many, many of them, some of the very best in fact, stopped practicing their faith entirely once they left the school. Even those from very strong Catholic families often went the same route.

I began to wonder if it was the peculiar nature of modern life that rendered it so difficult for young people to embrace the faith. Were the pressures from the world too strong for them? Was our goal indeed considerably less than realistic? I agonized over it. We all did.

I said we tried everything to help them come alive in faith. I actually should have said we did everything but evangelize them.

It was not until I began to evangelize my students that I commenced to see some of them touched deeply by the Lord. I was amazed at the faithfulness of God to move powerfully within the life of student after student. As they committed their lives to him, he honoured their decision by working an unmistakable transformation in them.

> *"To those who accepted him, he gave power to become children of God."* (John 1:12)

In the lives of those who committed themselves to him and trusted him, he acts. (Ps. 37:5) With those who opened the door, he came in, sat down, and had supper. (Rev. 3:20) To those who drew close to him, he drew close. (Jas. 4:8)

It happened. I am unable to deny what I saw. The Lord himself intervened in the lives of these young men and women. For many of them, the day they made a conscious choice for Jesus and his gospel was the turning point in their lives. And they remain faithful to him to this day. They didn't become perfect. But they certainly became different. And I became unalterably convinced that the first thing we must do for people, people of all ages, is evangelize them.

All the other things follow. Once they're evangelized, we can teach them, form them, help them grow in their faith, and prepare them to go out and touch a confused and broken world. Only where they are fully evangelized can they bring all the Lord's resources to the service of the poor, the respect-for-life movements, the organizations for justice, and the work for peace.

What opportunities there are to evangelize when we teach! What powerhouses our schools, in particular, could become! Even children can respond to the Lord, open their lives to him, and be dynamically moved. We must never underestimate the capacity of the young, even the very young, to respond to the Lord or place limits on what he can do to them.

Every teaching situation can and must be used to evangelize for the kingdom of God.

WITNESSING:

It is commonly felt by members of the Church that the work of evangelization belongs only to the clergy and religious. Not so. In fact, the commission to bring the Good News to the world was given by the Lord to the whole Church. We, the believers, are the Church. Whatever doubts we may have had about that were once and for all dispelled by Vatican II. While there is a special ministry of evangelization within the Body of Christ, a particular call and anointing to make a full-time work of calling others to faith, every Christian, every Catholic, is called by the Lord to be an evangelizer. This is what we call witnessing. We are all needed by the Lord as witnesses.

Many people will never get to hear the gospel summons from one of the Church's evangelists. For a vast number of the earth's inhabitants, the individual believer will be the only gospel they will ever read. Admittedly, this work of bringing the Good News of life on a one-to-one basis is fraught with hazard. Many have been turned off by well-meaning Christians who have attempted to witness them into a corner. Unless we do it right, with sensitivity, we can actually be doing harm.

I am reminded of the good woman who spoke to me once

about her unbelieving husband. "I'm so discouraged," she said. "I have tried everything, but I've got nowhere." As she explained to me what actually she had indeed done, I realized she was telling the truth. She had surely done everything. Maybe even more. She had left books open with passages underlined. She had placed religious tracts in strategic locations around the house. She had kept up an unending verbal witness. She had pasted Christian stickers all over the place. She had even glued one of the little fish symbols (early Christian sign for Christ himself) to her husband's shaving mirror. He wound up by cutting himself with his razor and blaming it, appropriately, on her and her "religious stuff". She could not understand why he would never eat fish after that!

This is a bit extreme. Not many Christian witnesses overplay their roles that badly. But it does represent a common enough mistake. We need the Lord's sensitivity. Not every person is ready all the time to hear the Lord's word. Not every situation is made to order for evangelizing. The Lord has a timing we must tune into. Too often we try to pry open the doors to people's lives. We must *pray* them open instead. A door pried open is a door damaged. If we beseech the Lord to open the door to someone's life, he will somehow let us know when it's open and the time is ripe for placing the Good News before the person who may now be ready to hear it. But we must have great patience. The Lord's timing and ours are not often the same.

Another thought. I know several believers who, every morning, ask the Lord to send them at least one person that day who is ready to hear the Word. And they invariable have a long list of heart-warming stories to tell of the people they have been privileged to lead to the Lord. Could we not all do the same?

I know that many members of the Church would plead inadequacy to the task. "We are not prepared or equipped for this," they might say. They might well be right. But we can't leave it at that. We have to get equipped.

We are not without resources. There are programs at hand designed to prepare evangelized believers to become evangelizers themselves. We are committed to sharing what we have been taught by the Lord with anyone anywhere and are open to inquiries.

A word of encouragement to parents. My work has brought me into contact with a great number of very discouraged people whose children have wandered away from the Lord in many directions. These are often pitiful and heart-rending stories. People ask themselves where they possibly could have gone wrong. They deeply rue the mistakes they believe they have made and continue to carry a heavy burden of guilt. And their present witness is of no avail and falls on deaf ears.

Parents need to be assured that the sins of their children are not to be laid at their doorstep. The pressures of this modern world, at the inspiration of the enemy himself, conspire with an unprecedented intensity to trap the young into patterns of life that have a terrible power to destroy them. Even the strongest of faith-filled homes are often no longer able to withstand the assault. In any case, the Lord has forgiven and forgotten all of our repented sinfulness. He's not interested in picking through the past. He's interested in the future. He is no accuser. Satan is our accuser, not our loving God.

The Lord wants us to know that what our efforts have failed to do, he will use our prayers, faithful and persevering, one day to accomplish. The writer of Psalm 37 says:

"If you take your delight in the Lord, he will give you the desires of your heart." (Ps. 37:4)

The deepest desire of believing parents' hearts is the salvation of their children. Let parents take their delight in the Lord, stay patiently in prayer, and trust God to accomplish what he has promised. He's reliable. I have seen too many lives of youngsters turned around to believe anything else.

Parents may not be around when it happens, but happen it will. Let them believe that, even if it has to be at some far-off place, perhaps after much suffering, their children will find the Lord. God wants us to *rejoice* now, take our delight in him, for what he will surely do.

7 THE FULLNESS OF SALVATION

The Christian Church is badly divided. This is one of the sad facts of life for us who belong to it. The divisions are a scandal and not God's doing. We have accomplished this all by ourselves. Our divided witness to the truth of the Lord's Word is the principal factor that robs our proclamation of the gospel of the power with which the Lord himself wants to endow it.

I believe it to be our bounden duty as members of the Church to unite with Jesus in his most fervent prayer:

> "I pray...that all may be one as you, Father, are in me and I am in you. I pray that they may be one in us, that the world may believe that you have sent me." (John 17:20-21)

I know the Lord is going to bring it about. It's in process now. Great things are happening in this direction and we can see them if we will ask the Lord for the eyes to see with. But as we persevere in prayer for this, work together in the ways we can, and patiently wait it out with him, we must seek every opportunity to broaden our mutual understanding of one another's positions.

This is an essay on evangelization. There are many Christian churches which bear the title "Evangelical", and others, like the Pentecostals who, though not titled as such, are evangelical as well. We need to understand what they're saying. They have, I believe, an important word from the Lord for us.

I've already pretty well said it all. The Evangelical churches would have little difficulty with most of the teaching on the preceding pages. They believe it is necessary for a person to make a conscious decision to embrace the Gospel, to choose Jesus as Lord and to accept the salvation he has won and made available. What we don't often realize is that this is also, of course, very Catholic. Although we don't generally evangelize as well as they do, our belief in the unique mediation of Jesus and the way the Lord has designed for us to enter into salvation is the same.

There are, we must confess, differences in our positions on salvation. But not as many differences as one might think. It is mainly *language* that makes our positions sound more different than they are. Reflecting on salvation for Nicodemus, Jesus said:

> *"Unless a man be born again of water and the Holy Spirit, he cannot enter the kingdom of God."* (John 3:5)

Catholics and Evangelicals both believe in the necessity of being born again. However, whereas we hold that this is a process that begins at Baptism and is advanced each time we respond to promptings of the Holy Spirit (actual graces we call them), the Evangelicals contend that being born again is a one-time experience. They take their lead principally from St. Paul's words to the Romans:

> *"If you confess with your lips that Jesus is Lord and believe in your heart that God raised him from the dead, you will be saved."* (Rom. 10:9)

In other words, when a person chooses Jesus as Lord and turns his whole life over to God, he becomes "born again" and is "saved". We believe, on the other hand, that this decision for Jesus is something that must be renewed again and again.

Actually, we think they should have a closer look at some of the other relevant scriptures. St. Paul says, for example, that

> *"...we are not saved yet..."* (Rom. 8:25)

He also says:

> *"I am racing to capture the prize (eternal life) for which Christ Jesus captured me."* (Phil. 3:12)

He tells the Galatians:

> *"If we don't give up the struggle, we should get our harvest"* *(membership in the heavenly kingdom).* (Gal. 6:9)

He makes the same point with the Philippians.

> *"Work out your salvation,"* he urges, *"in fear and trembling..."* (Phil. 2:12)

He would seem to be teaching us that, while our salvation has been won for us by Jesus, the price paid in full, we ourselves are on the way, in process. We will not, in other words, experience the fullness of salvation until we are with the Lord in heaven. We, therefore, must continue to respond to the Lord's will. We must persevere. The bottom line is doing the Father's will.

Jesus made it crystal clear.

> *"It is not those who cry 'Lord, Lord' who will enter the kingdom of God, but only those who do the will of my Father in heaven."* (Matt. 7:21)

He goes on to underline it by saying that even performing wonders through the power of the Holy Spirit will not qualify us for the divine household. Faithful obedience to the Lord is what he requires.

He says again:

> *"The one who stays faithful to the end is the one who will see salvation."* (Matt. 24:13)

The Catholic Church's reflection on all this is that salvation is for us, though assuredly a free gift, a process, a continual yielding to the promptings of the Holy Spirit, a persevering faithfulness to the will of God.

Thus, when an Evangelical asks me if I am saved, born again, I reply that I am being saved, being born again. What he really is asking me, in terms that I am familiar with, is whether or not I am in the state of grace, the state of friendship with God. The Evangelical is born again. The Catholic is in the state of grace. It is the same thing.

Most Evangelicals believe that salvation, once received, can be lost. So do we. They speak of being "backslidden". We call it "mortal sin". We both believe that "salvation" or the "state of grace" is regained through sincere repentance and confession.

Why, for them, the insistence on the one-time nature of salvation? It is simply a different theology, a different way of reflecting on God's action.

The point has already been made that, when a person consciously responds to the Lord's call to embrace the gospel, God himself moves him from within. The person senses God's action. He has an authentic religious experience. If this happens to be the first time he has felt the touch of God, everything seems different for him. All things become new. It is easy to understand why the one transformed is now referred to as "born again".

Evangelization, properly understood and carried out, produces an authentic experience of the Lord. It has been my observation that wherever a person is evangelized, there he will make his spiritual home. If we, as a Church, are not evangelizing fully, and we don't do much of it, many of our people will be evangelized somewhere else and leave the Catholic Church.

This is happening. Everywhere I have been in the past few years, Evangelical and Pentecostal congregations are expanding and parenting new churches. And, invariably, I'm told that their greatest area of growth is ex-Catholics.

Why do Catholics go to other churches? I would guard against an overly scientific analysis of the situation. If we think it is explainable as catering to emotions or a providing of simple answers we are missing the point. The principal reason the churches of an evangelical persuasion are growing is very simply that they evangelize.

I don't believe it is the Lord's will that Catholics leave their Church, but I think I can understand why they do it. They don't have a *good* reason, but they do have a *real* reason.

Indignation is not the response the Lord is looking for from us. The Lord doesn't want us to have our noses out of joint. He wants us to evangelize.

8 ALTAR CALL

There is one very concrete way of evangelizing, I believe, that the Lord wants us to learn from the Evangelicals. It is the altar call. After a preacher has proclaimed the Good News, he simply invites those who would like to respond to it to come forward and declare themselves to the Lord. It certainly isn't the only way to answer the Lord's call, but it does help.

I speak from experience here. I used a type of altar call with my Religion students. Having taught and explained all about the need to say "yes" to God's invitation to turn our lives totally over to him, I would give them a little print-out with a short text, a prayer of dedication in which they could, having decided to do it, vocalize their commitment to Christ.

Those who had chosen to make such a conscious decision, and I stressed the importance of giving it a lot of thought and prayer, would come to a celebration of the Eucharist, scheduled to fit into their various timetables. Just before Communion time, they would come forward, kneel, and read the prayer together.

Believe me—things happened. The Lord was consistently faithful to his promise to touch the lives of those who reach out to him. Lives changed. And stayed that way. I was witness again and again to genuine religious experience. The Lord was at work. He was doing what I had never been able to do —change people's lives.

I include here a couple of texts that I employed at different times. The first one is quite simple, but allows the responder quite clearly to turn his life over to the Lord.

> Dear Lord, I bow before you as the great God of heaven and earth and the loving Father of us all.
>
> Thank you for calling us to an eternal life of joy with you, made possible for us by the death of Jesus your divine Son, whom you have made King and Lord of all creation.
>
> Lord Jesus, I want to follow you completely. I want to turn away from all sinful patterns in my life. Help me to do this. I choose you as the only Lord and Saviour of my life and surrender everything to you—body and soul, mind and will, past, present and future, priorities and plans, and all my possessions. Deal with me in whatever way you wish.
>
> Come, Holy Spirit. Confirm me in my decision. Glory be...

The second one is somewhat longer and makes it possible for the person to do a bit more reflecting on some of the implications of handing his life over to God.

Father, I place myself in your presence now as I make this commitment that I believe your Son, Jesus, is calling me to make. Send your Holy Spirit upon me to help me to pray.

I worship you as Creator, God of heaven and earth, and I want to give you all the praise you expect from me.

My Lord Jesus, I want to follow your call. You have accomplished my salvation, and that of all the world, upon the Cross by the shedding of your blood. I accept that salvation.

You have died to take away the sins of the world. On the cross, you bore all of my sins, and your forgiveness is available to me. I confess my sinfulness. I claim that forgiveness, and I forgive all those who have ever offended me.

Jesus, it was out of love for all of us that you gave up your life. And you would have given it up out of love for me alone. I now accept that love.

I want you to be the Lord of my life in every possible way. I give you my understanding, my will, my spirit, my physical being, my possessions, my desires, and my plans. I want to surrender to you completely. I desire a personal relationship with you as my Lord and Saviour.

I give you my cares, my worries, my fears, my hang-ups, all my difficulties, and I ask you to set me free.

Father, my faith is weak. I want to believe, but doubts cause me to hesitate. Grant me, I pray, through Jesus, your Son, the gift of divine faith. Sweep away all my doubts and give me that assurance that only your gift of faith can impart.

Father, your Son, Jesus, said that if we asked you anything

in his name, you would faithfully grant it. I ask you now in Jesus' name to answer my prayer.

May all glory, all praise be to you, Father, all worship and honour, homage and blessing, and to the Son, and to the Holy Spirit, reigning with you, one God, now and forever. Amen.

I would caution against us thinking that there is something automatic about a particular set of words. It is not the formula that does the transforming, but God himself.

But it is a powerful dynamic. To put it crudely, it works. After all, Jesus did say:

> *"If you declare yourself for me before men, I will declare you before my Father in heaven."* (Matt. 10:32)

Jesus always means what he says and always follows through. There's something especially important about a public declaration for Christ. And the Lord always honours it. Although it has many forms and variations, it is commonly known as an "altar call".

There may be some people who are uncomfortable with the term. They may feel it has too "Protestant" a ring to it. I think we need to get over this kind of hang-up but, until we do, there's a perfectly good Catholic word that will do every bit as well. It is "consecration".

We mustn't let terminology hold us back. Whatever we are inclined to call it, let's do it.

9 LET'S GET
SERIOUS

Evangelization is the principal mission committed by Jesus to the Church. We may have to be reconverted to the task. Our priorities may have to be re-arranged.

I would not want to imply that we, as a Church, do not evangelize at all. We do. But we don't do a great deal of it. One of the main reasons we have been somewhat side-tracked is that we don't understand evangelization as well as we once did. The simple dynamic the Lord has given us has somehow slipped away from us to a great extent. We do have programs in many places that we call evangelization. But they do not all necessarily fit the description.

Most of our organized efforts to evangelize at present are aimed at bringing people to a position where they can be described as "practising" Catholics. We target two main groups: Catholics who are not attending church and others who belong to no church at all. On behalf of the former, the "lapsed" Catholics, different kinds of "welcome home" occasions and outreaches to the alienated are undertaken. In the case of the latter, the goal is to make "converts" to the Church.

Approaches and endeavours like these are good, entirely laudable and need to be encouraged. Would that they could be multiplied throughout the Church. But they are not evangelized. When we speak of the Church's prime mission to evangelize, we refer to bringing people into a personal and intimate relationship with the Lord, a relationship in which they can be said to know him and come to make his priorities their own.

St. John Paul II understood it well and taught it continually, and with great emphasis. He said that true evangelization draws forth a "sincere acceptance of the Good news" (Puebla, Mexico, 1980). And again: "God's action requires our response." (Ibid)

Why don't we listen more closely to the Pope? It has been my deep conviction for some time that we would be in far better shape as a Church than we are right now if we had been listening to the recent popes and been faithful to the direction they have been giving.

St. Paul VI understood what's at the heart of evangelization too. He spoke of the "radical conversion" (*Evangelii Nuntiandi*, 1975) that occurs through an authentic proclamation of the Gospel. He urged us not to forget that the people in the pews may well need to be evangelized as much as "fallen away" Catholics. He warned us that even the faith of those who come to church regularly can be largely cultural and formal and explained that a living faith requires a living relationship with the Lord.

Real evangelization, St. Paul VI said, will produce "a profound change of mind and heart." (Ibid 52) He spoke of our "need to know Jesus Christ." (Ibid 52)

St. John Paul II said "Let us seek the Lord. And once we have met him, let us remain with him." (St. Peter's, Rome, Feb. 1979) Evangelization brings us to a real *meeting* with the Lord, a meeting that touches us deeply and works a transformation in our lives. In the same address, the Holy Father urged us on: "Seek Jesus." He said. "Walk toward Christ. He alone is the solution to all your problems. He alone is the way, the truth and the life. He alone is the real salvation of the world. He alone is the hope of mankind." (Ibid) These are the words of one who knows what it is to evangelize. He stands among us today as the Church's main evangelist. Can we have any question in our minds what he meant when he used again and again as the watchword for the holy year: "Open wide the doors to the Redeemer"?

St. John Paul II consistently proclaimed very clear priorities for us. He stood faithful to the position that his predecessor, St. Paul VI, staked out for the Church when he said that evangelization "...constitutes the essential mission of the Church." (*Evangelii Nuntiandi* 14) In fact, he added that the Church "exists in order to evangelize." (Ibid)

The Church, the Body of Christ, has undertaken, in obedience to the instructions of Jesus, a wide variety of good and noble works. We gather people together to worship God. We visit the sick and the lonely. We espouse the cause of the disadvantaged. We lobby for life. We work for peace. We try to do what we can to balance the scales of human justice. We feed the hungry, shelter the homeless, clothe the naked. We teach. We minister to the wounded, the strays, the alienated, the imprisoned. And much more besides. This is only a partial list. Maybe we don't do them all as well as we should, and we need to have a good look at that. But our basic, primary call from the Lord is to evangelize and we must, without delay, restore it to first place.

Our dioceses and parishes have multiple ministries and services. We have qualified people responsible for Liturgy, Missions, Catechetics, Family Life, Social Justice, Administration and others. Do we have anyone for evangelization? Can we delay any longer in putting this in place?

We must waste no more time as a Church in becoming aggressively evangelistic. The Lord himself has given us a clear call. The popes have made it plain where they stand. Are we listening? Are we going to do it? We really have no choice. We have to.

We will never see the Church come vibrantly and explosively alive until we get serious about evangelization.

Also by Fr. Bob Bedard, CC

Give God Permission
The Memoirs of Fr. Bob Bedard, CC

The Catholic Disciple

We Are Called to be Companions of the Cross
Insights and Reflections on Our Life in Christ

FR. BOB BEDARD, CC
Courageous pioneer in the New Evangelization and Parish Renewal

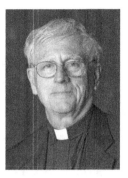

Fr. Bob Bedard (1929-2011) was the Founder of the *Companions of the Cross*. He came from humble beginnings in Ottawa where he was raised, went to school and was ordained a priest in 1955. He was a high school teacher for many years. Through his involvement in the Charismatic Renewal, the Lord transformed his ministry to his students and as a result many were evangelized and returned to their faith. His extensive speaking at conferences about the renewal of parishes had a tremendous impact and helped numerous people allow the Holy Spirit to be active in their lives. His open and surrendered approach to his faith throughout his life enabled him to say "yes", when the Lord asked for his permission to begin a new community of priests and seminarians in 1985.

In May of 2003 Archbishop Gervais issued the decree establishing the *Companions of the Cross* as a Society of Apostolic Life. In June of that same year the Servants of the Cross, a group of Sisters following the spirituality of the Companions of the Cross was begun.

The *Companions of the Cross* have foundations in Ottawa, Toronto, Halifax, Houston and Detroit.

For more information on our books, resources and Lay Formation programs, please visit: **companionscross.org**

A dynamic website with inspiring new content every day!

Sign up for our 'Best of the Web' email and subscribe to *Gaudium*—A magazine for the New Evangelization.

COMPANIONS OF THE CROSS

We are a community of Catholic priests inviting people to know Jesus and empowering them to share Jesus.

> *"I see the Church waking up and coming explosively alive to the point where it, with the power of the Holy Spirit, will shake the earth and the nations with its dynamic presence."* —Fr. Bob Bedard, CC

Our priests preach the Word of God with passion, celebrate the sacraments with devotion, and lead with confidence.

We root ourselves in:

Brotherhood
A LIFE OF TRUE BROTHERHOOD
We base ourselves on the model of Jesus and his disciples, who lived together, ministered together, and supported one another.

Spirituality
A SPIRITUALITY OF GOD'S POWER AND WISDOM
Jesus's death on the cross and resurrection saved the world. Therefore, we fully commit ourselves to him; seek his will in all we do; and trust in his power to carry it out.

Mission
A MISSION OF EVANGELIZATION AND RENEWAL
We invite all people into an initial and ongoing encounter with Jesus. As we are transformed by his love, we bring about authentic renewal in the Church and the world.

Follow Us:

199 Bayswater Avenue, Ottawa, ON Canada K1Y 2G5 | **1.866.885.8824**
info@companionscross.org | WWW.COMPANIONSCROSS.ORG